Online Jobs: How to be a Freelancer

A Guide to Freelance Jobs

By: Todd McLeod

TABLE OF CONTENTS

Todd McLeod
PUBLISHERS NOTES

Speedy Publishing LLC

40 E. Main St., #1156

Newark, DE 19711

www.speedypublishing.co

Cover Artwork: 24 Hr. Designs Ltd.

Editing: Speedy Publishing LLC

Book design: Speedy Publishing LLC

ISBN:

This is a reprint book.

DISCLAIMER

This publication is intended to provide helpful and informative material. It is not intended to diagnose, treat, cure, or prevent any health problem or condition, nor is intended to replace the advice of a physician. No action should be taken solely on the contents of this book. Always consult your physician or qualified health-care professional on any matters regarding your health and before adopting any suggestions in this book or drawing inferences from it.

The author and publisher specifically disclaim all responsibility for any liability, loss or risk, personal or otherwise, which is incurred as a consequence, directly or indirectly, from the use or application of any contents of this book.

Any and all product names referenced within this book are the trademarks of their respective owners. None of these owners have sponsored, authorized, endorsed, or approved this book.

Always read all information provided by the manufacturers' product labels before using their products. The author and publisher are not responsible for claims made by manufacturers.

Todd McLeod

DEDICATION

This book is dedicated to my family.

CHAPTER 1- FREELANCING – THE NEW WAY TO EARN MONEY

Whatever you do, do not start your hunt with any of the clients that you may have dealt with in your current job.

When you think of freelancing, what is the first thing that comes to your mind? You probably think of a writer, novelist or journalist right off hand.

That is primarily because for centuries, the only real job you could have as a freelancer had to do with your mastery of the written word.

But we are not still stuck back in the early nineteen hundreds – no we are in the twenty first century, a time that appreciates freelancers in hundreds of different jobs.

Sure, you have probably heard of freelance photographers too, you may have even met one or two in your life, but what about freelance software designers, freelance medical billing specialists, or even freelance scientific researchers?

There are all jobs that have recently begun to see massive growth in their respective fields because more and more people are realizing that they can make far more money working for themselves as freelancers than they ever could solely from working under the wing of their previous employer.

So it sounds pretty good doesn't it? You work in some field for quite a few years, get a lot of practical experience in your chosen area of employment and then gradually make the switch from working the nine to five to becoming your own boss as a freelancer.

But is it really as easy as it sounds to become a freelancer and actually make a living doing work on a freelance basis?

We have to keep in mind that there are quite a few freelancers out there who are only doing work part time.

Not because they make a ton of money and only have to work a couple of days per week but because they actually have had some trouble finding work in the past and need a much more solid career option in order to make sure that they do not find themselves facing bankruptcy.

However, such a scenario does not have to happen to you if you are willing to do whatever it takes to become a freelancer. Your career switch may not happen overnight – but eventually you will become highly successful at what you do.

It's a guarantee.

The first step in making that jump from office work to freelance is to decide whether or not you have what it takes to become a freelancer.

We all want to be our own boss, but do we all have the drive and dedication that it takes to be successful without the watchful eye of our supervisors?

Sadly, we don't.

Therefore, you have to really sit down and think about what makes you so special in the world of freelancers.

Do you have a large enough skill set to make you stand out amongst the hoards of different people all seeking the same work as you?

Do you have the time management skills necessary to run your own freelancing operation and meet all of the deadlines set upon you by your clients?

If you have even the slightest doubt in your mind about freelancing, then maybe there are other career paths that are better for you in the long run.

Now, provided that you are willing to jump in to your freelancing business with both feet, you need to start off on the freelance path slowly before you can really start raking in the cash.

Don't quit your job just yet! Instead, you need to begin your hunt for freelance work in your area of expertise on the internet and see what you can come up with.

Some skills, such as the ability to write coherently or do software design for clients of all types, are highly marketable and you should really have no difficulty whatsoever finding a goldmine of work.

On the other hand, if you are only able to do tasks that are not as easily marketable on a freelance basis, you will have much more difficulty finding work for your freelance operation.

Currently some of the most popular fields for freelancing include writing, editing, photography, web and graphic design, software design, and architecture or drafting.

Once you have settled on a field that you want to freelance in, you will need to start finding your first clients. Whatever you do, do not start your hunt with any of the clients that you may have dealt with in your current job.

There are all kinds of laws against this practice and it may get you into serious trouble if you are caught.

Instead, turn to your favorite search engine and search for some forums and databases specifically designed for freelancers seeking work in a particular field.

There are tons of different places for you to visit, so within an hour or so you will probably have at least ten or fifteen bookmarks of places online where you can find employment as a freelancer.

When you find you have some free time, all you have to do is search around on each one of these bookmarked websites to find the freelance positions that sound good to you.

When you start out as a freelancer, you will probably have to take a few jobs that do not pay very well at all. That's fine because these jobs help you build your skill set.

They will help you learn how to more effectively manage your time, speed up your workflow, and even help you get more used to using a computer and the internet to search for answers to any questions that may pop up while you are doing work for your client.

The low paying jobs will probably last for awhile, as until you have assembled a massive list of satisfied clients you will have to primarily compete with all of the other freelancers in your field entirely on how low your rates and fees are.

Eventually though you will graduate into higher and higher paying jobs until you will find that you have practically doubled your current income with income from freelancing.

At this point you should feel confident enough to possibly start thinking about reducing the number of hours you work at your current job to part time status or even quit your job all together and make your fortunes solely through freelancing in your selected field.

CHAPTER 2- THE ADVANTAGES AND DISADVANTAGES OF FREELANCING

You are in control of your work and nobody else (except for your clients) can tell you what to do.

After a long day at the office, you decide to stop by your local Barnes & Noble bookstore to pick up a copy of your favorite magazine.

When you open it up to a story that you find fascinating, you look at the author's name and see that in his biography it says that he is a professional freelance writer.

Looking at the selected photographs, drawings and diagrams quickly makes you realize that all of the artwork for the story was also done by freelance photographers and graphic designers.

Returning home from the bookstore, you decide to start up your computer and log online to check out the news for the day that you might have missed.

Topping the list on your favorite tech news website is a brand new program that looks like it could be a lot of use to you.

Visiting the software programmer's website shows that he is also a freelancer – and seems to be doing rather well at his chosen trade.

Realizing that so much is created by freelancers, you decide to dedicate the rest of your evening to researching the freelance databases to see if you have what it takes to join this growing world of self employed individuals.

Before you begin your hunt to be a freelancer though, you need to know the benefits and the drawbacks of working for yourself on a per client basis.

A lot of people will tell you that setting foot outside of the office was the best thing they ever could have done while others will tell you that they could not wait for each of their freelance projects to be over because they simply could not stand the stress of their assignments.

In order to be a successful freelancer you really have to weigh all of the pros and cons and be absolutely sure that the career path is right for you.

So, without further ado, here are some of the most common benefits and drawbacks you will face as a freelancer.

Advantages

The moment you decide to become a freelancer, everyone you talk to will probably tell you how cool it is to be your own boss.

You are in control of your work and nobody else (except for your clients) can tell you what to do. If you don't want to work on Fridays – you don't have to.

Take any days off that you want, but make sure that you finish your projects by the deadline. By being your own boss, you really have the freedom to steer your life where you want it to go.

You get to plan your own schedules, choose the projects that you find enjoyable, charge any rate you please, and be almost totally self sufficient – a major bonus of being a freelancer for many people looking to escape the daily grind.

Todd McLeod

Another of the big benefits you will always hear people talking about when it comes to freelancing is that you can set your own dress code. If you find all of your freelance work online, who is to say that you don't have to just hang around in your pajamas or underwear all day long?

No sense in getting all dressed up when you can just get out of bed, enjoy a nice cup of hot coffee, watch the news for a few minutes and then plop yourself down at your computer to start your workday.

Freelancing gives you the ability to work in your own style and in total comfort no matter who or what you are doing work for.

By working freelance you can also spend a lot more time with your family and friends.

Because you do not have to go to work on a strict schedule, you can spend time with your children when they get home from school and with your friends and your spouse whenever they have off work.

The flexibility of having a freelance career is second to none and there is practically no other job in the world that gives you both the spare time and the financial freedom to do what you want to do when you want to do it.

Finally, with freelancing you have a near limitless income potential. Because you work for yourself, you get to keep all of what you earn. Not a penny goes to anyone else (aside from the government in the form of taxes).

All of the profits belong to you so you get to spend it how you please. Furthermore, because you work on a per project basis, you can accept as many projects as you want to earn as much money as you see fit.

You are not salaried, so the more work you do, the more you get paid.

Disadvantages

As with anything in the world, there are drawbacks to becoming a freelancer in any field you choose. The predominant drawback is that you are not as financially stable as you are when you are working for someone else.

You have to take care of all of your money management, you have to work on project after project if you want to have enough money to stay financially afloat, and you have to provide for your own healthcare.

These three factors all add up to create a feeling of fiscal insecurity for many people, and because of the major financial risk involved, many people feel that freelancing is not for them.

There is also heavy competition in the world of freelancing. The internet has been both a blessing and a curse to freelancers from around the world.

On one hand it has opened the doors to make the world of freelancing much more accessible to anyone who has ever thought about setting out on their own and becoming their own boss.

On the other hand though, the internet makes it very easy for freelancers to get in touch with potential clients and possibly steal jobs right out from under you.

Todd McLeod

Because of the heavy competition as a result of the internet, you may have to start out with very low pay for each project you do as a novice freelancer.

When your client list expands however, you will be able to make more in the long term.

Chapter 3- How to Get Started Freelancing

Some potential clients may start coming to you with their work, hearing how much you can accomplish or how good you are at meeting deadlines.

We have all read an article, seen a photograph, tinkered around with some software, or visited a website that was designed by some type of freelancer.

Chances are that at some point or another we have all wanted to go out on our own – away from our current jobs – and start a new career path as a freelancer in our field of specialization.

But why don't we?

What holds so much of us back from going out and doing what it is that we want to do with our lives?

Why do we allow ourselves to be tied to our employer as if some invisible shackles enslave us?

What types of skills do we need in order to finally break free from the nine to five shifts and start out on our own as a freelancer?

You should ask yourself all of these questions before you even think about quitting your current occupation in pursuit of a freelance job.

Each and every year, far too many people believe that they can simply quit their jobs and pursue a career as a freelancer in whatever their specific field may be – and far too many of them fail, only to go crawling back to their previous employer in hopes that he will give the destitute freelancer his former job back.

This unfortunate circumstance happens for one reason and one reason alone – the person who wanted to branch out on his own as a freelancer had no idea what to expect.

People told him that he could be free, have as many days off as he wanted and retain all of the profits from his work.

But nobody ever told him that he may have to work long and hard to meet deadlines, manage his finances himself, and compete with thousands of others for the same clients.

Before you begin any ventures into the world of freelancing, you should know that it is not all fun and games – a lot of serious thought must go into your actions if you are to be successful.

Now that you have thought it over and you are absolutely sure that freelancing is right for you, it is time to set foot into your new career path and start looking for some work.

Whatever you do, do not quit your current job right now, as you will not have a livable source of income for at least a few months while you search for well paying projects.

Quitting your job will come in due time, but only after you have managed to net a few illustrious contracts first.

With your passion and desire in hand, the first step of your new life as a freelancer should be to log onto your computer, pull open your web browser of choice, head over to one of the top three search engines, and look for work.

Use specific keywords that can describe what you want to do with your life and sooner or later you will wind up with a massive database of different websites that cater to the freelance community in your specific field.

After all, if you are a freelance writer why would you look for work at the software programming freelance directories?

Once you have constructed a list of the top websites in your field where you think you will be able to find clients, visit the sites daily (or subscribe to their RSS feeds) to find projects that would not only be interesting to you but will also pay the bills.

Chances are that when you start out down the road of a freelancer in any field you will find that you can only get small time, low pay contracts and projects that really do not require much skill at all.

This is because you are new and relatively unknown to the freelance community.

As time passes though, and you get client after client, more and more people will start to know who you are and the kind of work you will do.

You can then net the higher paying projects that will allow you to really start supplementing your income greatly.

Eventually you may even find that some potential clients may start coming to you with their work, hearing how much you can accomplish or how good you are at meeting deadlines from the people who hired you previously.

Upon becoming a freelancer for the first time, it is also important that you create a mass of different items that can show off the kind of work you do.

Todd McLeod

Making this portfolio may be one of the most important things you can do if you want to succeed as a freelancer, as it will help you move up in the world of freelance work.

Only include projects that you have all of the rights to, as if someone thinks that you may have stolen pieces of your portfolio from others, the word may get out and you risk not being hired for freelance work by anyone – ever.

Furthermore, only add items to your portfolio that make you look good in whatever particular field you are trying to find freelance work in.

Sure, if you are looking for freelance work as a web designer you could include an article you wrote on chemistry, but why would someone looking for a skilled web designer really care about something you wrote for a chemistry website – unless your client was also hiring you to write his web copy.

Finally, your competition from around the globe will be another major barrier in your pursuit to become a self sufficient freelancer.

People from all walks of life and from just about every country in the world will be competing for the same projects as you, so you had better be prepared to offer something that other people simply cannot compete with.

For example, if you are a freelance writer or editor, the best way to compete is to explain to your clients that you are a native English speaker.

Graphic and web designers as well as software programmers should take plenty of extra college courses to show how well they are educated in their craft.

Finally, no matter field you are freelancing in, you should always take some time as an unpaid worker to create some examples for your portfolio that really highlight your strong points.

Todd McLeod

Chapter 4- How to Build a Customer Base

If you choose one of the popular freelance jobs, such as writer, editor, photographer, web designer, or software programmer then you will have a much easier time finding work online.

So you have finally decided to take that first big step in your career change towards the world of freelancing, but there is just one hitch – you have no idea where to find your first clients and customers.

A few years ago you would have to act solely by means of local businesses and private residents of your community in hopes that someone, anyone you know could lead you to a potentially high paying client for your freelance work.

Writers always had it easier because there were hundreds of magazines and newspapers who always needed freelancers on a day to day basis – but if you were a web designer or a software programmer, chances are you were out of luck. But that was back before the internet wove its way into homes across the world.

Finding customers for your fresh freelancing operation has never been easier thanks to the internet. People and companies looking for freelancer workers to help them with a project or two are all over the place and can help you get started in the freelance world if you are lucky enough to find a client that will work with you time and time again.

Furthermore, as a freelancer you can also use the internet to your advantage to advertise your services on various forums and other freelance web resources. In these situations, instead of you looking for some prospective clients, they look for you – allowing you to focus on whatever tasks and projects you are currently working on for others.

As an up and coming freelancer, the first thing you must do when looking for clients is to get your name out there. Let people know who you are, what you do, how well you do it, and what you can do for them.

Potential clients love a freelancer who is willing to get the job done right the first time on a timely manner, and if you have no prior experience, you may have trouble getting high paying customers to trust you right off the bat.

However, if you start with a few low paying jobs, you will quickly find that you can advance through the ranks very rapidly and soon be able to net all of the projects that will allow you to keep your freelance business self sufficient.

There is no better way to get off on the right path as a freelancer than to assemble a clear, concise, and focused portfolio of your work.

You can either include this portfolio as an email attachment when you apply for positions offered to you by clients, or if you have some web design skills you can create a personal portfolio website that outlines all of the specific projects that you have worked on over the years for various clients.

Whatever type of portfolio you choose to create, be sure that it is targeted to the audience you are trying to attract, as there is no sense in including work you did as a software programmer if you are looking for work as a freelance photographer for example.

Todd McLeod

Now, when it comes to finding clients for your freelance business in masses, you need to focus your attention to the various forums and discussion boards that dot the web.

Google is a great way to search for different websites that are specific to your chosen freelance field, and if possible you should avoid posting advertisements for your services in freelance forums that are not frequented by people who are looking for freelancers in your line of work.

Posting out of section makes you look bad and could result in you being banned from various freelancing websites that may have proven helpful to you in the future as your business expands.

Because it is so important for you to find freelance websites that are focused to your particular field of operation, you need to decide on one or two services that you think you can find freelance work in and then go from there.

If you choose one of the popular freelance jobs, such as writer, editor, photographer, web designer, or software programmer then you will have a much easier time finding work online because there are so many different freelance directories available to you.

As any kind of freelancer, one of the best places to start your search for customers from around the world is Craig's List.

This is your one stop shop that can help you find work in your local metro area as well as in cities and countries from around the world.

Most of the jobs offered at Craig's List allow you to work at home although you may have to visit the offices of some of the higher paying positions from time to time.

Another amazing resource for freelancers of all kinds is Guru, a website that helps prospective freelancers in all fields find customers from around the world.

It caters mostly to well establish freelance professionals though, so you may want to turn to it later once you have exhausted your other freelancing options.

If you are a freelance writer or editor, there are a couple of excellent freelancing websites for you.

The first is Freelance Writing, a massive database where employers and freelancers can post their information in hopes that they will find a suitable match on a per project basis.

You will mostly find lower paying jobs here, but it is a great start if you are just getting into freelancing or if you are simply looking for a couple of easy part time projects to supplement your current income.

Also, the Writer's Market is a great place to not only find work but to learn all of the ins and outs of the writing and editing business. You can get in touch with potential clients as well as hone your skills as a writer.

Those involved in the world of design and programming should turn to ScriptLance as their source of well paying jobs in their chosen industry.

As one of the leading websites for those involved in programming and design, this is probably the most likely place that you will find a well paying job in the web and software field. If you are looking for other options, check out the Freelance Job Search, a website that will help you find lesser known, but well paying freelance jobs in the world of web design, graphic design, and programming.

CHAPTER 5- DOES IT REALLY MAKE SENSE TO FREELANCE

The first thing that you have to realize about being a freelancer is that you may not be able to make ends meet.

If you are planning to quit your current job and enter the world of the freelancer, then you had better be pretty darn well sure that this is something you want to do.

Even if you are totally sure that you want to become a freelancer in your chosen field, is it something that is financially possible for you?

Can you support your family on the salary you make from a freelancer?

What about healthcare, are you prepared to give that up too in pursuit of a future as a freelancer?

Can you handle the stress that comes from working with tight, often ridiculous deadlines on your projects?

Do you work well by yourself and can you speak well when talking with a potential client who may want to hire you for his next project?

Finally, do you have what it takes to constantly advertise yourself and your services to anyone who may be interested?

Far too often, people think that they want to be freelancers simply because it sounds cool.

After all, many people get it into their heads that there is no more relaxing work atmosphere than being able to wake up late, work on your computer while you are wearing your pajamas, and take off whatever days you want as your vacation.

Sure, those are all perks of being a freelancer, but let's be honest here - there are quite a few trials and tribulations that you will have to go through as a freelancer before you can reach the point where you do not have to worry about your finances anymore.

Yes, that is something that so many people fail to realize – you cannot expect to simply quit your current job for life as a freelancer and suddenly have hundreds of potential clients knocking at your door in hope that you will do a project for them.

There is much more to freelancing than that, so let's find out if you have what it takes to make it in the cutthroat world of the freelancer.

The first thing that you have to realize about being a freelancer is that you may not be able to make ends meet on freelancing alone for quite some time.

So, if you are thinking about quitting your current job – don't do it just yet. Instead, test the waters and be sure that you like freelancing first, and find out how much money you can make as a freelancer before you even begin to work on your resignation papers.

As a fledgling freelancer, your best bet is to start off with clients that may not pay as much but will be able to get you in the door.

Sure, you will have to take jobs that you may think are below you – but in the end it will pay off.

Maybe not financially at first, but by way of getting your name out there and adding employment opportunities to your ever expanding list of satisfied customers.

Therefore, if you want to freelance professionally, you have to be willing to take a pay cut at first in order to be successful later.

Secondly, you have to figure out whether or not you can support your family on the salary you will make as a freelancer.

Remember that you will have to take a pay cut from your current job when you first start out as a freelancer, and when you finally quit your current job for good, will you be able to bring in enough work to keep your family's lifestyle at the same level it currently is?

These are important questions that you have to ask yourself before you make that big leap into the world of freelancing.

While it is not very important if you decide to keep doing freelance work as a supplement to your current income – it will become extremely important if you decide to make your freelance salary your sole income.

Next, you have to think about what you will do for healthcare as a freelancer. Without the support of an already established business behind you, you will have to pay for your own (and your family's) health insurance out of pocket.

This is not a big deal if you have a spouse that gets health insurance from his or her workplace, but if your spouse is a stay at home parent or is involved in their own freelance business, this becomes a major expense to think about.

So be sure that you will be able to afford health insurance for all of your loved ones when you become a freelancer.

Stress management is a key factor of working for you as a freelancer. You will be faced with projects that may require you to work long and hard before you can finish them.

Often, these projects will be extremely difficult and be under some ludicrous deadline – making them that much more intense. So, are you good at handling stressful situations such as these?

After all, if you are not able to get the project back to your client on time and in working order, you may be discredited and have a much more difficult time finding work for many months to come.

Are you a team player or do you work better as an individual? While this question may seem insignificant, remember that as a freelancer you really have no team to rely on should you not know how to do something.

Sure, you could scour the internet for answers to your questions – but that will take away valuable time from your project.

So, if you are the type of person who can accomplish tasks more efficiently in a group, then you may want to rethink the idea of going freelance, because the individualize work environment of a freelancer is certainly not for you.

Finally, can you handle the fact that you must constantly advertise your services to just about anyone who may need you to do some work for them?

Do you have enough self esteem that you can promote yourself as if you are the best freelancer out there?

Being able to constantly advertise your services is a major benefit for anyone looking to become a freelancer.

Todd McLeod

While it is possible to by shy or withdrawn and be successful at freelancing, you will have a much easier time if you are more vocal about promoting your services to prospective customers.

ABOUT THE AUTHOR

Recent years has seen a massive surge in online job posting websites where the average Joe can apply to an entire range of jobs that can all be carried out from the comfort of your own home. Todd McLeod went through the process from applying to landing the perfect job as a freelancer. Jobs can vary from virtual assistants to web-based researchers, videography to photography, or if you would prefer to simply write content and leave the technical stuff to the professionals, you could try and make money writing articles or reviews, or even use your creative mind and get paid to write short stories.

The possibilities are literally endless when it comes to writing online for a living. Test the water and sign yourself up to as many job-posting websites as you feel necessary. Simply prepare your personal profile, update your CV as much as you can and start applying to as many positions that you think may suit your skills. If you don't apply yourself, nobody else will do it for you. Grab a copy of Todd's book!

www.ingramcontent.com/pod-product-compliance
Lightning Source LLC
Chambersburg PA
CBHW051420170526
45165CB00004BA/1893